Natural Numbers

An Arkansas Number Book

Written by Mike Shoulders and Illustrated by Rick Anderson

Sleeping Bear Press™

310 North Main Street, Suite 300
Chelsea, MI 48118
www.sleepingbearpress.com

© 2008 Sleeping Bear Press is an imprint of Gale, a part of Cengage Learning.

Printed and bound in China.

First Edition

10 9 8 7 6 5 4 3 2 1

Library of Congress Cataloging-in-Publication Data

Shoulders, Michael.
Natural numbers: an Arkansas number book / written by Michael Shoulders;
illustrated by Rick Anderson.
p. cm.
Summary: "Arkansas facts, symbols, geography, and famous places are
introduced using numbers. Learn about 1 Pivot Rock, 3 ivory-billed woodpeckers, 8 square dancers, 20 pine trees, and more. Each topic is introduced
with a poem, followed by detailed side-bar text"—Provided by publisher.
ISBN 978-1-58536-172-4
1. Arkansas—Juvenile literature. 2. Counting—Juvenile literature.
I. Anderson, Rick, 1947- ill. II. Title.
F411.3.S564 2008
979.1--dc22   2008009661

To the faculty and staff of Charleston Elementary School—
a great place to learn to read

MICHAEL

In loving memory of my mother,
Juanita Anderson.

RICK

Pivot Rock, an unusual geological formation, sits deep in a wooded area of the Ozark Mountains in northwestern Arkansas not far from the town of Eureka Springs. The top of Pivot Rock is 15 times wider than the base and is large enough to hold a bus. Local legend says the Jesse James gang used the vicinity of Pivot Rock for their hideout.

Although referred to as the Ozark Mountains, this area is actually an eroded plateau carved over thousands of years by creeks and rivers. Many of the mountains in the Ozarks are nearly the same height. This is a telltale sign this area was once a plateau and that water eroded the land to form mountains.

Residents and tourists have visited this area for over a hundred years, not only to view Pivot Rock but to take in the beauty of the surrounding area. Visitors walk wooded trails, cross a natural bridge, and explore caves. Nature's beauty is on full display in this part of the United States, showing why Arkansas is nicknamed "The Natural State."

one
1

1 huge rock looming tall
makes eyes stare, open wide.
"Pivot Rock" stands on a point
instead of resting on its side.

The city of Texarkana spans two states: Arkansas and Texas. There is a city government for each state. What makes this town unique is that the post office and courthouse sit in two states. No other post office in America spans two states. The post office's address is Texarkana, Arkansas-Texas. This building even has two zip codes: 71854 for Texarkana, Arkansas, mail and 75501 for Texarkana, Texas, mail.

The two states worked together to build their courthouse and post office. Texas supplied pink granite for the base and Arkansas supplied limestone for the walls.

Because of its unique location, visitors straddle a line outside the post office in "photographer's island" to get a picture showing they stood in two states at one time. The Texarkana courthouse may be the second most photographed courthouse in the United States, second only to the Supreme Court in Washington, D.C.

two
2

2 states merge in Texarkana
in the middle of Main Street.
A line outside the town's post office
shows where these two states meet.

TEXARKANA

TEXAS

STATE LINE

ARKANSAS

At 20 inches long, the ivory-bill is America's largest woodpecker. They are black and white with large white triangles on each wing. The male's crest is red, while the female's is completely black. Ivory-bills got their name from the color of their bills.

The ivory-bill is partial to tracts of uncut, mature timber and usually feeds on beetles and larvae found in dead trees. They also eat acorns, grapes, persimmons, and black gum berries. The bird's decline over the last 50 years was blamed on logging of bottomland forests.

Since the last confirmed sighting of an ivory-billed woodpecker (*Campephilus principalis*) occurred in Cuba in 1987, scientists thought these birds were extinct. The last sighting of an ivory-billed woodpecker in the United States was in 1944! However, Gene Sparling, paddling a kayak in the Cache River National Wildlife Refuge in eastern Arkansas, spotted an ivory-billed woodpecker on February 11, 2004.

three
3

3 ivory-billed woodpeckers—
their markings are distinct!
Not seen in America for 60 years,
they were thought to be extinct.

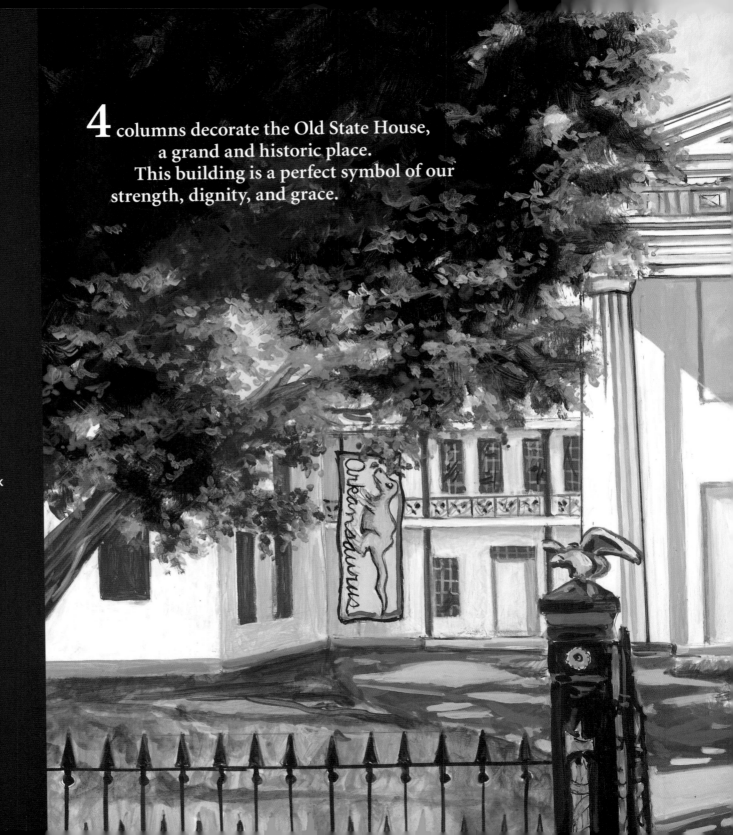

Construction on Arkansas' first capitol began in 1833 at 300 West Markham Street, Little Rock. It officially became Arkansas' capitol in 1842, when legislators first met there. The Old State House is an *antebellum*, meaning built before the Civil War. It is the oldest surviving state capitol west of the Mississippi River. This building served as Arkansas' capitol until 1911 when government offices moved a little over a mile away to what is now Capitol Avenue.

In 1947, the Arkansas legislature turned the Old State House into a museum. It houses exhibits on Arkansas. One room showcases the history of the building. Another room features the history of Arkansas' women including Patsy Montana, the first female singer to sell a million records with "I Want to Be a Cowboy's Sweetheart."

The four columns featured on the front of the Old State House are characteristic of an architecture style called Greek Revival, meaning imitating ancient Greek forms.

four

4

4 columns decorate the Old State House,
a grand and historic place.
This building is a perfect symbol of our
strength, dignity, and grace.

5 fiddlers gather on a porch
and rosin up their bows.
They jam to "Turkey in the Straw"
as they wait to begin a show.

Because of its close association with Arkansas folk music and culture, the state legislature adopted the fiddle as the official state instrument in 1985. *Jam* is a musical term meaning an impromptu performance. A jam session is often comprised of people who have never played together before. During old-time fiddler's competitions, small groups of musicians may gather wherever they can for jam sessions.

What is the difference between a violin and fiddle? Sometimes, a violin has an arched bridge to allow the player to play one string at a time. Generally speaking, performers consider the violin and fiddle the same instrument.

Rosin is made from tree sap. Fiddlers apply it to the hairs of a bow. As fiddlers pull the bow across the strings, rosin grabs the strings to create a clear pitch. If there is not enough rosin on the bow, it slides across the strings without producing a tone.

five

5

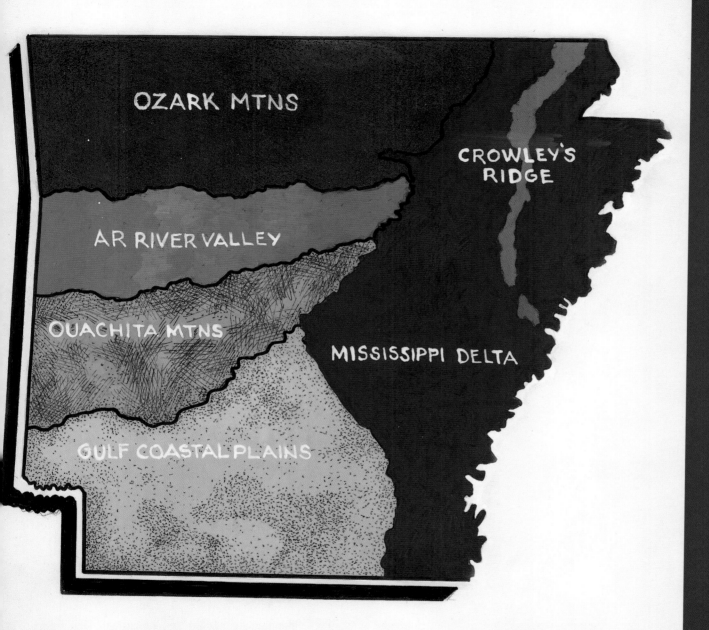

Ozark Mountains—Streams carved through here 300 millions years ago to form these flat-topped mountains. This area includes rough terrain, rock formations, towering bluffs and limestone caves. **River Valley**—Roughly 40 miles wide, this area contains pines, swamps, bottomland forests, and hardwood trees. Large cities are found here. **Ouachita Mountains**—Pine forests cover much of these mountains. Thermal springs and the diamond crater at Murfreesboro are located here. **Gulf Coastal Plain**—Long ago covered by the Gulf of Mexico, today this area supports agriculture and provides much needed oil and natural gas.

Delta or Mississippi Alluvial Plain—In eastern Arkansas this area features farmlands, swamps and rich soil, supplying much of the agricultural products for the state. **Crowley's Ridge**—The Mississippi and Ohio Rivers formed Crowley's Ridge when their courses shifted millions of years ago. This long, narrow chain of hills is 4 to 5 miles wide and 150 miles long.

six

6 natural regions form Arkansas. They're different yet all contain resources providing work and play from mountains to coastal plain.

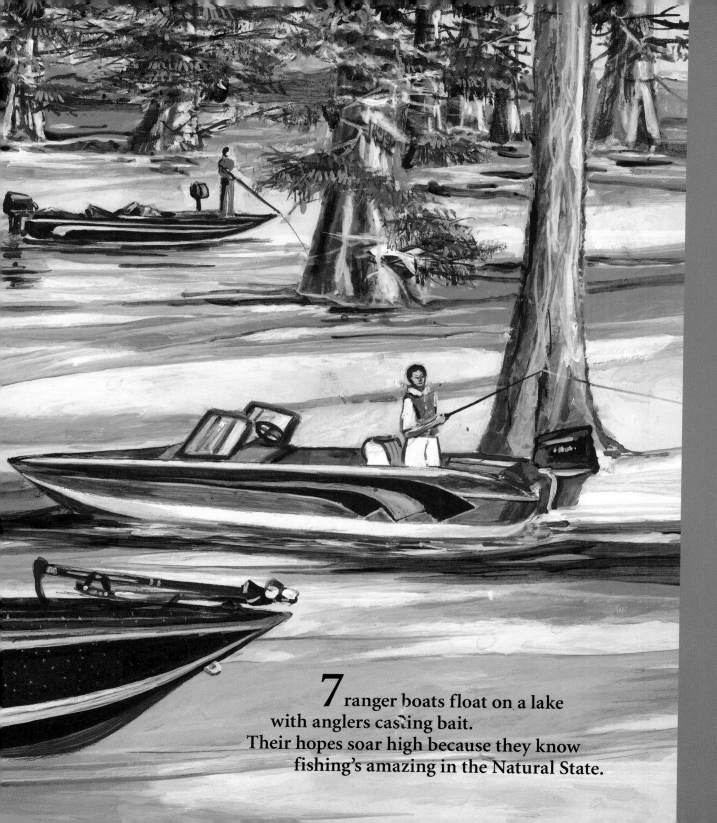

Arkansans love outdoor activities! No wonder Arkansas is called "The Natural State!" Since many fish year-round, it's no surprise that a resident built a company providing millions of people a way to enjoy all types of water recreation. Forrest L. Wood founded the Ranger Boat Company in Flippin, Arkansas in 1968. Today the company has grown into a major Arkansas industry producing over 40 different models of boats for any water activity. People use Ranger Boats for fishing, skiing, tubing, hunting, or just relaxing a lazy day away on rivers and lakes.

seven

7

7 ranger boats float on a lake
with anglers casting bait.
Their hopes soar high because they know
fishing's amazing in the Natural State.

8 square dancers dressed to the nines,
the ladies in calico.
"The Men Star Left. The Girls Swing Thru.
All partners do-si-do."

The square dance became Arkansas' official state American folk dance in 1991. In a square dance, eight people work as a team called a square. Their objective is to complete a set of complex routines chanted to them by a "caller." All this is done while music plays in the background.

Callers sometimes choreograph their routines in advance. But often their calls are "off the cuff" or spontaneous. Either way, the square has to listen carefully because dancers never know what the caller is going to call for them to do. Traditionally, callers begin and end with "bow to your partner" and "bow to your corner." Square dancers usually "Dress to the nines" meaning nearly to perfection!

Dance steps have fun names:
Dixie Diamonds
Do-si-do (pronounced *doe-see-doe*)
Scatter Scoot
Star Left
Teacup Chain

eight
8

9 rainbow trout swimming in a river
may soon be someone's meal.
Grab some bait, some fishing line,
and your rod and reel!

Trout fishing was virtually nonexistent in Arkansas fifty years ago. After World War II the Army Corps of Engineers built dams and created Norfork and Bull Shoals Lakes. Other dams followed in the 1960s. Since rainbow trout prefer cool, clear water between 55 and 60 degrees Fahrenheit, the cold-water runoff from the dams is perfect.

In 1957 the Norfork National Fish Hatchery was created. Today in-state hatcheries produce more than 2,000,000 trout for release in Arkansas' waters. These trout are released when they reach 9 inches in length.

The White River is more than 700 miles long and flows past Cotter. Since it is home to many fishing resorts and fishing guide services, anglers come from all over the world to try their fishing luck here.

The state record rainbow trout of 19 pounds 1 ounce was caught in the White River in 1981.

nine
9

Evidences of Indians living in Arkansas dates back 10,000 years. Indians used paints made from charcoal, blood, animal fat, egg whites, plant oil, and other substances to create images on cave walls. They often used frayed twigs or fingers for paintbrushes. Early native drawings depicted humans, animals, sunbursts, as well as geometric and abstract designs.

Cave paintings are still visible at many sites across Arkansas including at the state's first state park, Petit Jean State Park. Most of the rock art found in Arkansas is believed to be between 600 and 1,100 years old.

Carbon dating helps determine when cave art was drawn. Scientists compare the amount of carbon-14 to the amount of carbon-12 in things that were once alive, such as berry juice, bones, or wooden utensils to determine its age. In 5,700 years, half of the carbon-14 decays in living things, while carbon-12 remains exactly the same. Determining the exact ratio of carbon-14 to carbon-12 gives scientist a good idea of an object's age.

ten
10

10 rock paintings left in a cave
present a mystery.
Were they drawn for fun, to tell a story,
or record Indian history?

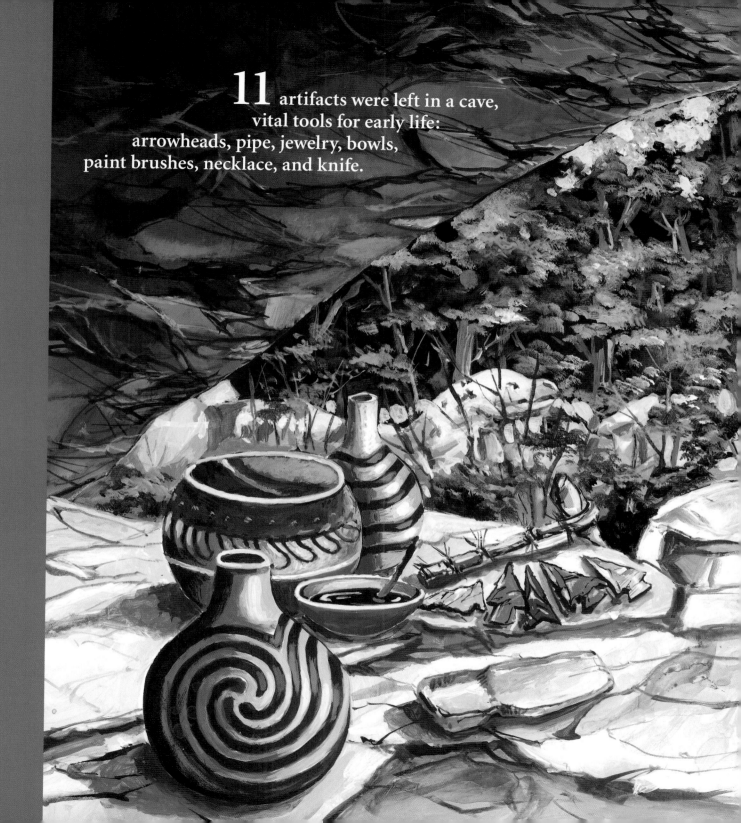

Artifacts have been called "windows to the past." Artifacts are objects such as tools, pieces of pottery, jewelry, or weapons that were made by people who lived before us. We learn about previous peoples from what they left behind. Art and artifacts help paint a picture of how people lived, what they hunted, and what they valued. Many artifacts, such as bowls and knives, helped sustain life. Some artifacts, such as jewelry, show us how early Arkansans adorned themselves.

Bluff shelters at Petit Jean State Park, about an hour northwest of Little Rock, housed Native Americans thousands of years ago. Their existence in this area is evidenced by pictographs left on the walls of Rock Horse Cave.

By learning about the past we make connections between our lives and those who lived here before us.

eleven

11

11 artifacts were left in a cave,
vital tools for early life:
arrowheads, pipe, jewelry, bowls,
paint brushes, necklace, and knife.

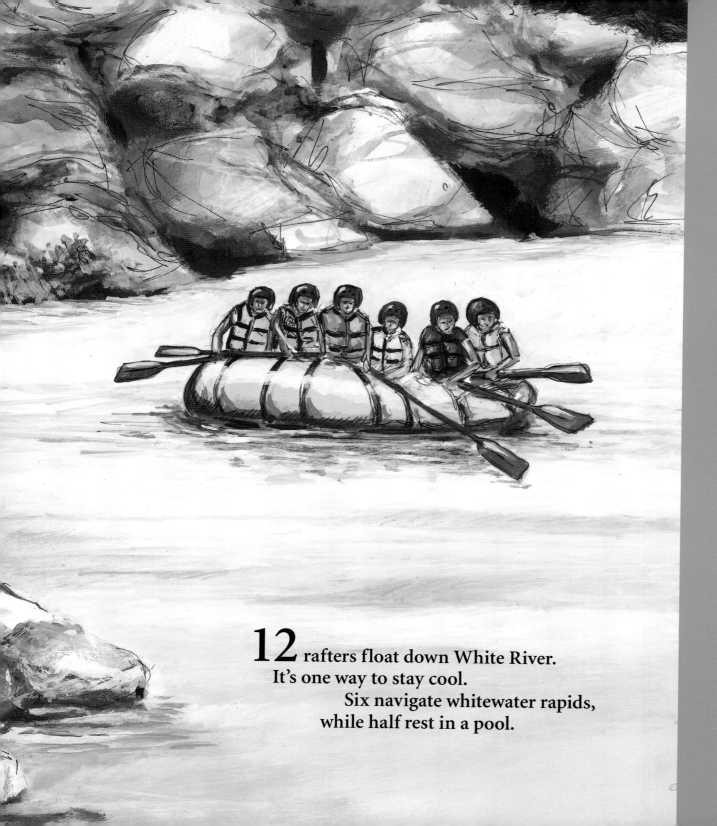

Long ago, the Ozark Mountains isolated the people of northern and western Arkansas from the rest of the state. Today that is no longer true. Resorts near clear water lakes and rivers, including the White River, draw vacationers from all over America to this part of the state. While there, they enjoy canoeing, hiking, biking, camping, and fishing.

One popular summer activity is floating down the White River on inner tubes or rafts. This is one way to cool visitors during Arkansas' long hot summer days.

Batesville is home to the White River Water Carnival held every year in August. The first celebration was in August of 1938. Today this festival features arts and crafts, concerts, beauty pageants, car shows, and concludes with a grand parade and firework display.

twelve

12

12 rafters float down White River.
It's one way to stay cool.
    Six navigate whitewater rapids,
    while half rest in a pool.

The Fifty-Second General Assembly of Arkansas named the pine the official state tree on January 20, 1939. Pine trees are evergreens, meaning they stay green all year. Cones grow on pines and range from four to eight inches long. Several types of pine trees can be found in Arkansas but the loblolly (*Pinus taeda*) is the most common. The state's legislature, when they designated the pine as the official state tree, did not name a specific pine. The short-leaf pines, slash pines, and long-leaf pines are commonly found across the state.

Pine trees are considered by some to be the most important commercial tree grown in Arkansas. They are widely used to make furniture, paneling, fence posts, and flooring. Pine pulp is used to make paper.

Pine trees may grow to 120 feet tall.

twenty
20

20 trees against a sky of blue
create a striking scene.
Pines stay green all year long
so we call them *evergreen*.

30 cows chew their cuds each day
through 90 pounds of food!
The end result is our state drink,
natural, wholesome, and good.

Holstein cows are black and white and make up more than 90% of dairy cows in Arkansas. Holsteins weigh approximately 1,400 pounds when fully grown.

Cow Facts:
- Cows drink up to 40 gallons of water a day.
- Cows eat up to 90 pounds of food a day.
- Cows give 200,000 glasses of milk in a lifetime.
- Every day 9 million cows are milked in the United States.
- A cow chews her cud (regurgitated food) for up to 8 hours each day.
- A cow's udder holds up to 50 pounds of milk.
- Most cows give about 6.5 gallons of milk per day.
- The highest producing cows give over 25 gallons or 400 glasses a day.

Milk has been called nature's most nearly perfect food. Since dairy farming is an important part of Arkansas' agriculture, milk was chosen as the official state beverage in 1985.

Many years ago, travel on the Arkansas River was unpredictable. It might overflow its banks one month and be too shallow for boats the next. Today, sixteen locks and dams divide the Arkansas River into a series of "pools" to make travel possible all year.

When the river was low, crews waited in Conway. "Toad Suck Daze," celebrated the first weekend in May, honors those thirsty crews.

Toad competition rules:
- Only toads may compete.
- Toads cannot be prodded, pushed, thrown, or shoved.
- Toads may not be touched other than placed back in their lane if they hop out of bounds.

What's the difference between frogs and toads? Toads have shorter legs and hop. Frogs jump. Toads live on land while frogs live in water.

forty
40

40 toads, ready to compete.
All sizes big and small.
Their legs are short so they don't jump.
Instead, they hop or crawl.

50 tracks preserved through time
were left along a shore.
Arkansaurus fridayi
was a vicious predator.

Paleontologists frequently unearth complete dinosaurs in the western half of the United States. Such finds are rare in the eastern half. Why? Roads, cities, buildings, and an abundance of vegetation often conceal their remains.

In 1972, J. B. Friday discovered a foot bone, three claws, and two vertebrae from a dinosaur while looking for a lost cow in Lockesburg, *Arkansaurus fridayi*, pronounced AHR-kan-SAWR-us, was named for its discoverer. This meat eater lived approximately 70 million years ago during the last part of the Cretaceous Period.

We learn about dinosaurs by studying their fossil remains. Dinosaurs became fossilized when they were buried in sand or mud soon after death. Bacteria destroyed their fleshy parts but left their bones and teeth. With just a complete foot, scientists know Arkansaurus was carnivorous. They also know it walked on hind limbs and had shorter fore limbs.

fifty
50

Arkansas leads the nation in the production of rice. Try this tasty recipe for crispy rice cereal snacks.

Ingredients:
6 cups crispy rice cereal
3 tablespoons margarine or butter
7-ounce jar marshmallow crème

1. Measure cereal into large bowl.
2. Spray end of spatula & baking pan with nonstick cooking spray.
3. In a bowl, melt butter in microwave for about 30 seconds.
4. Add marshmallow crème to melted butter and mix with mixing spoon.
5. Pour the mixture over the cereal and stir with spoon until well coated.
6. Pour cereal mixture into baking pan. Press mixture evenly with spatula.

(optional)

7. When slightly cooled, cut mixture with buttered cookie cutter.
8. Press two identical shapes together with a popsicle stick between them.
9. Allow shapes to cool completely.
10. Make faces with almonds, raisins, red hots, and cake decorator icing.

sixty
60

60 snacks of crispy rice
make delicious sticky treats.
They're fun to make, easy as pie,
and ohhh so good to eat!

70 bottles at Quigley's Castle
make rainbows out of trees.
Evil spirits are caught inside each one
as they ride by on a breeze.

Elise Fiovanti began collecting rocks as a schoolgirl. At the age of 18 she married Albert Quigley and brought her rock collection to their new home site near Eureka Springs, Arkansas. For three years she covered the outside of her "castle" with the rocks she had collected over the years.

Elise continued adding to her castle over the next 50 years. For instance, she used empty bottles to make 14 bottle trees. Bottle trees, an ancient African tradition, date back to ninth century Congo. African legends say evil spirits are drawn to the splash of color and become trapped inside the bottles. Listen carefully when the wind blows past a bottle tree and the spirits' voices can be heard moaning from inside.

Bottle trees were once made by stripping the leaves off tree branches and replacing them with colorful bottles. Cedar trees worked best because their branches point upward and hold bottles easily.

The Mississippi flyway, a 3,000-mile route taken by migratory birds, begins in the Arctic Circle and stretches all the way to the Gulf of Mexico. This flight pattern brings many birds straight over Arkansas where they stop to eat and rest. For this reason, Arkansas attracts bird hunters wanting to try their luck.

Since Arkansas is an important part of the Mississippi Flyway, it's only natural that the World's Championship Duck Calling Contest is held every year in Stuggart, Arkansas. Ducks make different sounds for different situations. Therefore, contestants must perform four different calls in 90 seconds including a "feed call" which hunters use to lure ducks with the promise of food. The "come back call," an urgent sound, brings ducks back if they try to fly away from the hunter. The World's Championship Duck Calling Contest began in 1936.

eighty
80

80 snow geese heading south
stop in the Natural State.
They fly right over Arkansas
and rest as they migrate.

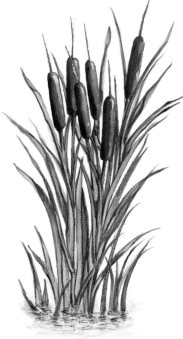

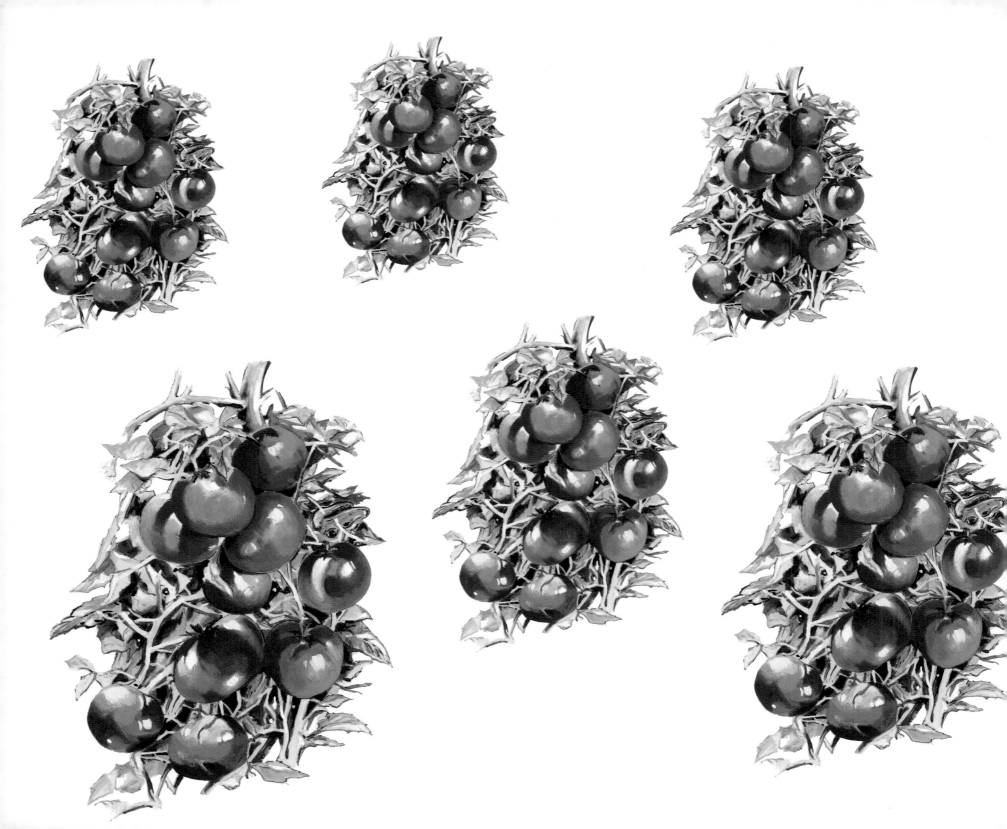

90 vine-ripe pink tomatoes—
they're our official state fruit.
Some have argued they're a vegetable.
The Supreme Court settled that dispute.

Fruits are the edible parts of the plant that contain the seeds. Vegetables are edible stems, leaves, and roots of a plant. So, biologically, a tomato is a fruit. Because of this discrepancy there have always been arguments whether the tomato is a fruit or vegetable. On May 16, 1987, the Arkansas state legislature said that since the tomato is a fruit but is used as a vegetable, the South Arkansas vine-ripe pink tomato should be the state's official fruit and vegetable, the only state to classify it as both.

In 1883, imported tomatoes were taxed as vegetables. Some argued tomatoes were fruits and should not be taxed. The Supreme Court ruled that since the public views tomatoes as vegetables, the court would do the same.

- Tennessee named the tomato as their official state FRUIT.
- New Jersey named the tomato as their official state VEGETABLE.

ninety
90

Because of its importance, the apple blossom was named Arkansas' state flower on January 30, 1901. At that time Arkansas was one of the leading producers of apples in the United States and was called "The Land of the Big Red Apple." Benton County was the chief apple-producing county in the United States. Today Arkansas ranks 32nd in the United States in the production of apples.

It is believed Jonathan Chapman, better known as Johnny Appleseed, first brought apple trees to Arkansas. The town of Lincoln hosts an Apple Festival each year.

Apple blossoms have pink and white petals and appear on apple trees in spring. However, the blossoms soon fall off and apples can grow where the blooms once appeared.

one hundred 100

100 apple blossoms create
a patch of pink and white.
When our state flower is in full bloom
nature paints an awesome sight.

Michael Shoulders

Having been involved in education in many different roles for more than 30 years, Dr. Michael Shoulders travels extensively, visiting schools, speaking at conferences across the country, and spreading the word that "Reading Is Magic." He has written several books for Sleeping Bear Press including the companion title, *N is for Natural State: An Arkansas Alphabet,* and two about his home state of Tennessee: *V is for Volunteer: A Tennessee Alphabet* and *Count on Us: A Tennessee Number Book.* Mike lives in Clarksville, Tennessee with his wife, Debbie.

Rick Anderson

After teaching art in the classroom for 25 years, illustrator Rick Anderson shares his talents with children and adults alike in picture books. *Natural Numbers* is Rick's fourth book with Sleeping Bear Press and is the companion title to *N is for Natural State: An Arkansas Alphabet.* Rick, who holds a master's degree in art education from Delta State University, travels the country visiting schools, conducting workshops, and speaking during reading conventions and other literacy events.

His work has been included in such prestigious juried shows as the Rocky Mountain National Watermedia Exhibition, the Southern Watercolor Society, the Mississippi Watercolor Society, the Rutgers National Drawing Show, the Maryland National Waterfowl Exhibition, and won "Best of Show" at the Gum Tree Festival in Tupelo, Mississippi. Rick lives in Clinton, Mississippi, with his wife, Merrie. For more about Rick visit rickandersonart.com.